OCT - 2017

Dangerous Jane

To my good friend, Donna Riemer,
who has a heart for helping others.

—S. S.

In loving memory of my mother, who
cherished her vocation as much as she adored
her students, and had the exceptional ability
to recognize the purpose in every child and
inspire them to change the world.

—A. R.

Dangerous Jane

Suzanne Slade

Illustrated by Alice Ratterree

PEACHTREE
ATLANTA

Jane was born

beside a sparkling creek

on an Illinois prairie

in a friendly town called Cedarville.

Her mother died
when she was only two—
much too young to understand
why Mama never came back,
but old enough to know
deep sadness and pain.

Then a disease made
Jane's back crooked,
her toes point in.
She felt like the ugly duckling
in her storybook:
different,
unwanted,
hopeless.

Jane had few friends, but she always had her father.

The two read piles of books together,

went on long walks,

and enjoyed trips into town to see their favorite sights.

One day, Jane and her father

passed through the poor side of town,

filled with new sights she'd never seen:

small, rundown shacks,

sad, hungry parents,

cold, barefoot children.

Jane's heart ached,

a strong, familiar ache.

She knew how it felt to be

sad,

rejected,

without hope.

Jane wanted to help those families.

But their problems were too big

for a small girl to fix.

So Jane promised herself—

when she grew up,

she would buy a big house

to share with people in need.

The years passed quickly—
time for Jane to leave home,
get married,
and start a family.
That's what women
were supposed to do.

But Jane had plans of her own—
college, and a career helping others.
She studied hard,
graduated at the top of her class,
and set off to learn about the world.

Jane saw statues in Italy,

operas in France,

and castles in Ireland.

But in England,

she saw something quite different:

starving people

spending their last pennies

on rotten vegetables.

Jane felt that familiar ache in her heart.

Poverty seemed to be everywhere.

How could she help?

Then she heard about Toynbee Hall—

a settlement house in London

that helped poor people help themselves,

by providing skills, confidence, dignity—

a new start in life.

So Jane visited that house

where guests learned to read and write,

discovered art and history,

attended concerts and classes.

And it gave her an idea!

Determined to keep her long-ago promise

to help struggling families,

Jane set sail for home,

dreaming of her own settlement house,

where immigrants who worked

too-long days,

at back-breaking jobs,

for next-to-nothing pay,

could find help.

Jane searched Chicago

and found a big, brick building

in the perfect place:

near families in desperate need.

But the old house was far from perfect.

Broken windows.

Peeling paint.

Crooked doors.

Undaunted, Jane traveled all over town,

asking wealthy women for donations

to turn this broken-down building

into a home—

a settlement called Hull House.

In 1889, Jane swung the front doors wide open.

Everyone was welcome. Anytime.

Working eighteen hours a day,

she provided whatever her neighbors needed:

English lessons, childcare, washtubs, steady work.

But most important,

she gave friendship, dignity, hope.

Families flocked to Jane's big house—

immigrants from Italy, Greece, Russia,

Ireland, Germany, Poland, and more.

Sometimes they argued

about beliefs and ideas.

So Jane asked them to listen carefully,

respect one another,

and peacefully settle their differences.

And everyone at Hull House got along fine.

Neighbors called her
"Miss Kind Heart."
Newspapers named her "Saint Jane."
President Roosevelt wrote her
a letter of "sincere thanks."
The *New York Evening Post* even
wanted Jane to run for President!

But while Jane was talking peace,

Europe was talking war.

Countries argued

over land, money, and power.

They built weapons and trained armies.

On July 28, 1914,

Jane read the horrible news—

World War I had begun!

Within days, more nations joined in,

to help their friends,

to defend their land,

to protect their citizens.

It seemed everybody loved Jane—
at Hull House,
in Chicago,
across the country.

Many soldiers died in the brutal battles.

Families were forced from their villages.

More people than ever were homeless. Starving.

Jane's caring heart ached like never before.

It ached for the world.

For twenty-five years,

she'd helped people from different countries

live in peace at Hull House.

But what could Jane do to stop a war?

Jane knew exactly what to do!

She brought women across America together

to form the Women's Peace Party

and find a way to end the war.

Overseas, women heard about Jane.

They longed for peace too,

so they organized a gathering in the Netherlands.

The International Congress of Women

needed a brave leader.

They needed Jane.

Jane joined fifteen hundred women
from twelve countries,
all determined to work together for peace.

The women debated for days,
searching for bold new ways
to stop the war.

They created twenty resolutions—

ideas for peace—

to share with world leaders.

Newspapers called their plan "silly."

Women cooked, cleaned, and cared for children.

What could women say

to presidents and prime ministers?

Jane knew what to say.
War-weary, road-weary,
she crisscrossed fourteen countries.

She shared her peace resolutions
with the British prime minister,
the French foreign minister,
the Austrian prime minister,
and even the Pope.

Jane understood war was complicated,
but she believed each idea,
each visit,
each smile and handshake,
made another small step toward peace.

She penned hundreds of letters,
led peace conferences,
and pleaded with warring nations
to talk to each other,
and more importantly,
to listen.

After four bloody years,

the war ended in 1918.

Finally,

peace.

No time to rest.

Jane packed her bags. Again.

Sailed across that ocean. Again.

Her tired heart was breaking for faraway neighbors

in war-torn countries.

She visited children in hospitals

and fed starving families.

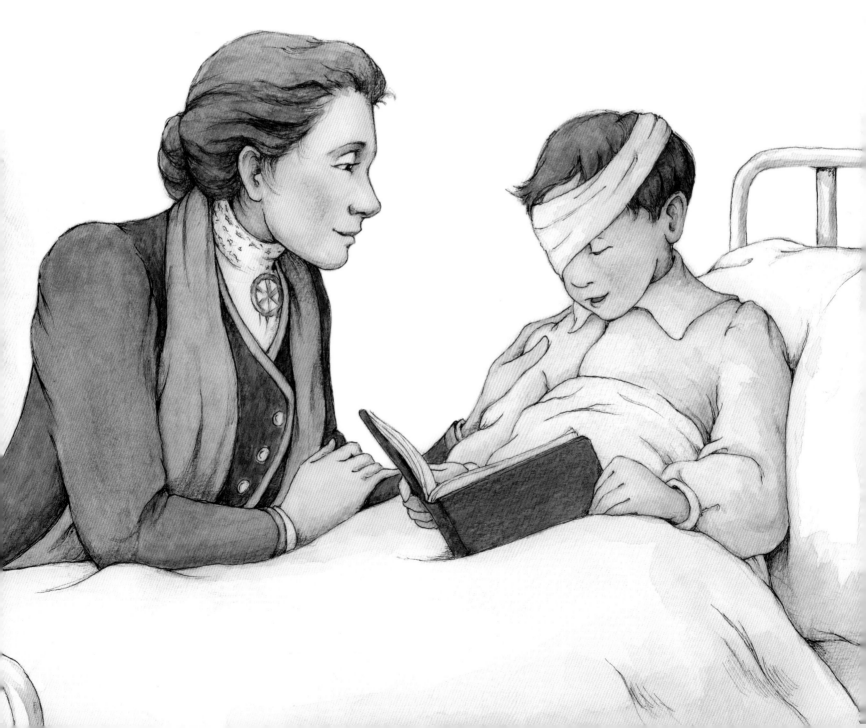

Back home,

some people didn't like who Jane helped—

strangers in other countries.

Or how Jane helped them—

giving away precious food!

Dark lies swirled around her
like an angry tornado.
Some said Jane was a traitor!
Did she care more about former enemies
in faraway countries
than her own neighbors next door?

Jane received nasty letters
from people around the country,
people she'd never even met.
When she gave speeches,
the crowds that once loved her
booed her off the stage.

Then the FBI named Jane
"the Most Dangerous Woman in America"!
What would Jane do now?

Jane kept doing what she'd always done:

helping people.

No matter where they were from.

No matter what others thought.

No matter what the cost.

Year

after year

after year.

But something changed in 1931.

Dangerous Jane was given a new name—

Nobel Laureate.

Jane Addams

was the first American woman

to win the Nobel Peace Prize!

Jane had never paid much attention

to what others said,

or the names people called her.

She just kept right on working

for world peace,

for people in need,

for the rest of her life.

"Nothing could be worse than the fear that one had given up too soon, and had left one effort unexpended which might have saved the world."

—Jane Addams

More about Dangerous Jane
(and her other names)

Jane Addams devoted her life to helping others—the poor, the homeless, and the hungry. Determined to help those without a voice, she also fought for rights for women and African Americans, and even took on corrupt politicians. A prolific author, she wrote eleven books about democracy, education, and peace. She was known by many names: leader, pioneer, pacifist, humanitarian, servant of the poor, champion for democracy—but no one ever expected she would be called "Dangerous."

When Jane founded Hull House (named after Charles Hull, the man who built the building) with her college friend Ellen Gates Starr, immigrants from thirty countries lived in her Chicago neighborhood. Those families worked long days at low-paying jobs, yet they couldn't afford heat or running water, and they had no access to public schools. Jane worked to improve the quality of their lives by providing classes such as English, cooking, and science, along with social events. Jane also served as encourager, peacemaker, and friend to her guests.

After keeping the peace at Hull House for twenty-five years, Jane was grief-stricken when World War I began. So she gathered women from across America to create the Women's Peace Party, then headed to the Netherlands to work with women from twelve countries at the International Congress of Women. To get there, she had to cross the English Channel, a very dangerous war zone.

The women delegates passed twenty resolutions. One, called the "Conference of Neutrals," proposed that neutral countries lead peace talks between the warring nations.

When the conference ended, Jane and other women set sail to share their ideas. Women from neutral countries visited the leaders of countries at war. Women from warring countries visited neutral countries. Many leaders agreed with the resolutions, but change was slow and the war dragged on. Jane continued her peace efforts until the war ended in 1918.

After the war, some Americans began to question Jane's loyalty because she'd encouraged Hull House guests with many different political views to speak out. On top of that, she was helping people overseas who'd been enemies during the war. As lies grew and fear overtook the nation, the FBI named Jane "the Most Dangerous Woman in the America." Yet, the truth prevailed and twelve years later she became the first American woman to win the Nobel Peace Prize!

During her seventy-four years, Jane helped countless people. What makes her achievements even more astounding is the fact that she battled health problems for much of her life. At age four, spinal tuberculosis curved her spine. She later endured pneumonia, kidney problems, a heart attack, cancer, and more. Despite her suffering, Jane never stopped working for peace and helping others.

Timeline

1860	Laura Jane Addams is born in Cedarville, Illinois, on September 6.
1863	Jane's mother dies.
1865	Jane contracts what doctors believe to be tuberculosis of the spine.
1866	On a business trip with her father to a town called Kilgrubbin, Jane sees rundown shacks and announces she will buy a big house someday to share with poor families.
1877–1881	Jane attends Rockford Female Seminary, where she meets Ellen Gates Starr.
1888	Jane visits Toynbee Hall, the world's first settlement house, in England.
1889	Jane and Ellen Gates Starr open Hull House, a settlement house in Chicago.
1902	Jane publishes her first book, *Democracy and Social Ethics*.
1906	President Theodore Roosevelt sends Jane a letter of thanks.
1906	Jane publishes *Newer Ideals of Peace*.
1909	Jane helps found the National Association for the Advancement of Colored People (NAACP).
1913	Woodrow Wilson becomes president of the United States.
July 28, 1914	**World War I begins.**
1915	Three thousand American women meet in Washington, DC, and form the Woman's Peace Party. Jane is elected president.
1915	Jane leads 1500 women from twelve countries at the International Congress of Women in the Netherlands.
1915	Jane travels to Europe to share peace resolutions with leaders of fourteen warring countries.
April 6, 1917	**The United States enters World War I.**
November 11, 1918	**World War I ends.**
1919	Jane raises money to send food to starving children overseas and visits children's hospitals in Germany.
1919	Jane founds the Women's International League for Peace and Freedom (WILPF) and becomes their first president.
1919	The FBI names Jane "the Most Dangerous Woman in America."
1929–1939	**The Great Depression**
1931	Jane becomes the first American woman awarded the Nobel Peace Prize.
1935	Jane Addams dies in Chicago, Illinois, on May 21 at age 74.

Opposite page:

Jane Addams at age 70

Left:

American delegates to the International Congress of Women, on board the Noordam. Jane Addams is third from left.

Selected Bibliography

Addams, Jane, *Peace and Bread in Time of War.* New York: Macmillan, 1983.

Addams, Jane, *Twenty Years at Hull-House.* New York: New American Library, 1953.

Addams, Jane, *The Second Twenty Years at Hull-House.* New York: Macmillan, 1930.

Addams, Jane, Emily Balch, and Alice Hamilton, *Women at the Hague.* New York: Macmillan, 1915.

Bryan, Mary Lynn McCree, Barbara Bair, and Maree De Angury, eds., *The Selected Papers of Jane Addams Vol. 1.* Urbana: University of Illinois Press, 2003.

Bryan, Mary Lynn McCree, Barbara Bair, and Maree De Angury, eds., *The Selected Papers of Jane Addams Vol. 2.* Urbana: University of Illinois Press, 2009.

Deegan, Mary Jo, *Jane Addams and the Men of the Chicago School.* New Brunswick, NJ: Transaction Books, 1986.

Fradin, Judith Bloom, and Dennis Brindell, *Jane Addams, Champion of Democracy.* New York: Houghton Mifflin, 2006.

Lynn, James Weber, *Jane Addams, A Biography.* Urbana: University of Illinois Press, 2000.

Lipsky, Mortimer, *Quest for Peace: the Story of the Nobel Award.* New York: A. S. Barnes and Co., 1966.

Sources for Quotes

page 19   "Miss Kind Heart," "Saint Jane": *Jane Addams, Champion of Democracy,* p. 95

page 19   "very sincere thanks": January 24, 1906 letter from President Roosevelt to Jane Addams (accessed at Hull House Museum)

page 27   "silly": *Jane Addams, A Biography,* p. 300

page 38   "Nothing could be … saved the world.": *Quest for Peace,* p. 138

Photos on pages 38 and 39 courtesy of the Library of Congress.

Acknowledgments

With gratitude to the Jane Addams Hull-House Museum staff—Lisa Junkin Lopez, Heather Radke, Rachel Shrock, and Michael Ramirez—for their gracious assistance in my research. Also, special thanks to Wendy E. Chmielewski, PhD., Curator of the Swarthmore College Peace Collection, for sharing her expertise.

—S. S.

My sincere appreciation to the University of Illinois at Chicago's Office of Facility & Space Planning and Special Collections & University Archives for sharing their research with me. Thank you to my agent Marietta B. Zacker for her wonderful encouragement.

—A. R.

Ω

Peachtree Publishers
1700 Chattahoochee Avenue NW
Atlanta, Georgia 30318-2112
www.peachtree-online.com

Text © 2017 Suzanne Slade
Illustrations © 2017 Alice Ratterree

Editor: Kathy Landwehr
Art Director: Nicola Simmonds Carmack
The illustrations were rendered in watercolor.

Printed in March 2017 by Tien Wah in Malaysia
First Edition
10 9 8 7 6 5 4 3 2 1
ISBN 978-1-56145-913-1

Library of Congress Cataloging-in-Publication Data

Names: Slade, Suzanne, author. | Ratterree, Alice, illustrator.
Title: Dangerous Jane / written by Suzanne Slade ; illustrated by Alice Ratterree.
Description: First edition. | Atlanta, GA : Peachtree Publishers, 2017.
Identifiers: LCCN 2016026430 | ISBN 9781561459131
Subjects: LCSH: Addams, Jane, 1860-1935—Juvenile literature. | Women social workers—United States— Biography—Juvenile literature. | Women social reformers—United States—Biography—Juvenile literature.
Classification: LCC HV40.32.A33 S595 2017 | DDC 361.92 [B]—dc23 LC record available at https://lccn.loc.gov/2016026430